First Edition 2013
Published by Destinworld Publishing Ltd.
www.destinworld.com

British Library Cataloguing-in-Publication Data
A catalogue record for this book is available from the British Library.

ISBN 978-0-9567187-4-7

Design by John Wright

CONTENTS

ABOUT THE AUTHORS   3
INTRODUCTION   4
1. HISTORIC   7
2. DOMESTIC   31
3. MILITARY   51
4. HELICOPTERS   67
5. CARGO   73
6. CHARTER/VIP   93
7. BIZJETS   101
8. AIRPORT   115
9. JUHU AERODROME   127
10. INTERNATIONAL   133

JIMMY WADIA

Jimmy Wadia, born in Bombay in 1949, took an early interest in aviation from his school days. His first encounter was in 1962, when strolling down the South Bombay roads. He glanced on an aircraft book entitled 'The Observers Book of Aircraft'-1962 edition, by William Green, and he made his decision to buy the 'Observers' as well as the monthly 'Air Pictorial', which he collected for over 30 years. Next, a Boy Scout picnic to Bombay Airport catapulted him into the true aviation world... there was no turning back, and he visited the open air gallery at Santa Cruz Airport regularly! He contributed articles to 'World Airline Fleets' in the seventies and joined 'Air-Britain (Historians) Ltd' in 1980. He also compiled the VT- registers for 'JP Airline Fleets' for several years. The airport authorities at the then Bombay Airport allowed him exclusive airside access as an official photographer on many occasions, when he literally roamed the ramp on his own!

But, as all good things come to an end, terrorism changed everything. Security became an issue at airports the world over. In Jimmy's words "Once aviation enters your bloodstream the show must go on."

SEAN DSILVA

Based in Mumbai, Sean found in himself an intrepid zest for airplanes right from infancy. His mother would take him on numerous evening sojourns to the airport as a toddler. His first birthday cake was even a poor replica of an Air India L-1011 Tristar! Throughout his childhood and his college days Sean would frequent the airport for hours on end, jotting down registration details, colour schemes, and various special sightings the old fashioned way - pencil... notebook... binoculars!

Sean freelances as an aviation photojournalist and spottographer – a term he coined to encompass plane spotting with airplane photography! His photographs have been featured in several international aviation publications including books, magazines, journals, and aviation photography websites. He was one of the winners of the Volga Dnepr 20th anniversary special aviation photography competition held in 2010. Sean specializes in chronicling air traffic movements at his home airport, Mumbai - the airport he holds very close to his heart.

MUMBAI AIRPORTS

Mumbai, a cosmopolitan city and the economic lifeline of India, spans over a land area of 600 square kilometers. It is home to over 15 million inhabitants, speaking a variety of different languages - the principal of which being Marathi. However, English is widely spoken and is the medium of education in most schools and colleges. Being on the coast of the Arabian Sea, the climate of Mumbai is very much influenced by the sea.

Before Mumbai there was Bombay, and in many parts of the city, and in peoples' hearts, that is what she will always be. But Mumbai, Bombay, Bumbai, Bombao - whatever you call her - this city fills its part of the world unforgettably.

Mumbai is accessible by various means of transport. The most prominent of which is the Chhatrapati Shivaji International Airport (CSIA), a gateway to the city from where all domestic and international operations are flown. Mumbai can be reached from practically anywhere in the world by air. Another small airport, the Juhu Aerodrome, only a few kilometers away from CSIA mainly serves general aviation and helicopter operations for offshore duties.

JUHU AERODROME
ICAO Code: VAJJ
OWNER: AIRPORTS AUTHORITY OF INDIA
The airport at Juhu was in the past India's premier civil airport; founded in 1928 as Vile Parle Flying Club, and known as Juhu, a name derived from the residential suburb alongside the vast sandy beach on the Arabian Sea. Initially operations commenced from an unpaved airfield, until two runways 08-26 and 16-34 were laid in 1936. The former is the main runway, measuring 3,750ft, while the second runway, 16-34, is only 2,400ft. Just 25km from the city centre, Juhu is spread over 400 acres with an elevation of just 20ft. The airport is managed by the Airports Authority of India.

The Bombay Flying Club (BFC) was the first to set up on the grassy airfield, surrounded by palm trees and a cool breeze all day long from the nearby Arabian Sea. BFC was incorporated as a limited company on 9th May, 1928. The club's first aircraft took to the air from Juhu on 13th January, 1929. As the club's membership grew to 127 members by 1929, training started in earnest, and the variety of aircraft the club used for training and pleasure flying included Gipsy Moth, Major Moth, Tiger Moth, Moth Minor, Chipmunk, Piper Super Cruiser, Super Cub and the Sentinel L-5. The BFC also owned DH Vega Gull, Argus, Beech Bonanza and an Auster Autocar. Today, BFC flies Cessna 152A aircraft, acquired from the Aero Club of India.

It was on the 15th of October, 1932, when the doyen of Indian aviation JRD Tata created history at Juhu, flying in a Puss Moth from Karachi to Bombay via Ahmedabad, thus marking the beginning of civil aviation in India. He repeated this feat 50 years later, but in a Leopard Moth (VT-AKH). The 1932 flight was the birth of Tata Airlines, which later became Air India. Initially, Tata had its first office in the shape of a palm-thatched hut at Juhu Aerodrome.

Besides the BFC, Indamer Company, India's first MRO organization was founded by an aviation minded American, Joseph Koszarek, in 1947 - Ind for India, and Amer for America. Situated in Hangar No. 1 at Juhu, Indamer commenced operations with just five employees. This has grown to over 500 today, and has completed more than 65 years at the same location. Initially Indamer Co. was the authorized sales and service centre for Hawker Beechcraft Corporation, and it was a pleasure to glance at a variety of Beech aircraft parked on the Indamer ramp and at their hangar undergoing overhaul. Today, Indamer has become the authorized service centre for the Brazilian Company - Embraer Aircraft Corporation. Joseph's son Richard carried on his father's business with equal zeal and devotion, but with changes everywhere, Indamer also changed hands.

The Oil and Natural Gas Commission (ONGC) has a large helicopter base at Juhu, from where it carries men and material to offshore oil rigs at the Bombay High oilfields. ONGC has time and again leased choppers from various foreign sources – Schreiner Helicopters, Okanagan Helicopters, Houston Helicopters to name a few, as well as Russian types. However, Pawan Hans Helicopters (previously Helicopter Corporation of India) is the main helicopter service provider for ONGC at Juhu today. Other smaller operators include Deccan Charters, Heligo Charters, King Rotors and Air Charter, Global Vectra Helicopters and United Helicharters.

Juhu served as the city's primary airport during and up to World War II, until Santa Cruz Airport, now CSIA, was built in 1948. As Santa Cruz Airport is within a 2 km radius of Juhu Aerodrome, the proximity of the two airports caused much confusion among pilots in the early days, and there are three known instances when pilots have mistaken the Juhu's 08-26 runway for Santa Cruz's 09-27 and have made unintended landings. These were:

1. A de Havilland DH-106 Comet 1 of BOAC (G-ALYY) landed on the Juhu runway on 15th July, 1953. Luckily, there were no fatalities. The aircraft was flown out nine days later, albeit with reduced weight.

2. On 24th September, 1972, a Japan Air Lines Douglas DC-8-53 (JA8013) operating as flight 472 made the same mistake. The aircraft was damaged beyond economic repair.

3. Almost three months later, on 14th December, 1972, an Interflug Ilyushin IL-18 also landed on Juhu's 08-26 runway.

Like all airports around the world, Juhu has been given a stringent security cover with armed guards at its entrance, and fencing around the perimeter. Gone are the days when one used to enter the airfield and give a smile to the lone security guard at the gate who would reply with a wave. Gone are the days when you can wander round the airfield on your own. Also gone are the days when children from the nearby airport colony and the adjoining slums would enjoy a game of cricket on the airport grounds at sundown, when Juhu goes to sleep.

CHHATRAPATI SHIVAJI INTERNATIONAL AIRPORT

IATA: BOM
ICAO: VABB
OWNER: MUMBAI INTERNATIONAL AIRPORT LIMITED (MIAL)

Chhatrapati Shivaji International Airport (CSIA) is also known as Santa Cruz Airport, and Sahar International Airport by the locals, due to its proximity to the suburbs of Santa Cruz and Sahar. It is one of the few airports in the world which falls within the municipal limits of the city it serves, and is only 25km from the city centre, surrounded by both high-rises and slums; a growing divide between the city's affluent class and the poor.

The airport is the primary international airport of Mumbai. It is named after the 17th century Maratha Emperor Chhatrapati Shivaji Bhosle, and is one of the busiest and largest airports in Asia, spread over an area of 4,800 acres. It has two intersecting runways; the main runway is 09-27, aligned east-west, and is 3,445m (11,302ft) in length, with a width of 60m (200ft). The other, smaller runway 14-32 measures 2,925m (9596ft) and is 45m (148ft) wide. Both runways have been upgraded to Code F, which enables them to accommodate the largest aircraft in passenger operation – namely the Airbus A380. During peak hours, both runways operate simultaneously. Passenger movements during the year April 2011 to March 2012 was 30,747,841. Cargo tonnage was 657,470, and aircraft movements were 251,492 during the same period.

CSIA is currently undergoing a major revamp, with new terminals, new taxiways, rapid-exits from the runways, and even a new control tower which stands 275ft tall - the second tallest in India. It is being built opposite the existing Terminal 1B, in a section of the parking lot. The old tower, which is in close proximity to runway 14-32, will be demolished shortly.

A BRIEF HISTORY...

As the nearby Juhu Aerodrome (VAJJ) was facing operational difficulties, with growing traffic, and constant flooding during the monsoon months, it was felt there was a need for a new airport. In 1942, an airfield was built within the municipal limits of Bombay in the suburb of Santa Cruz, spread over an area of 200 acres; it came to be called Santa Cruz Airport. During the Second World War the British based several Royal Air Force (RAF) squadrons at the airport, leaving in 1947. During the early years, Santa Cruz was far removed from the hustle and bustle of city life and was surrounded by green vegetation. After the withdrawal of RAF, the British handed over the airport to the Director General of Civil Aviation (DGCA) for civil operations, and the two hangars abandoned by the RAF were converted into passenger terminals. One hangar was used for domestic passengers, and the other for international operations with its own customs and immigration facilities.

After the partition of the sub-continent, and with Karachi going to Pakistan, traffic at Bombay Airport saw an increase with as many as 40 flights a day. It was thus becoming increasingly difficult for the two vintage hangars to cope with the traffic, and a new terminal building, control tower and apron was constructed on the opposite side of runway 09-27. A Fire Station later sprang up opposite the terminal building. Travellers in those days will well remember the raising of the red/yellow chequered flag over the tower, which signalled either an arrival or a departure. An open-air viewing gallery with a small cafeteria was a welcome move for visitors and enthusiasts alike. The viewing gallery was initially free of cost and was open 24 hours, 7 days a week, since most international services served Bombay during night hours.

The old RAF hangars gave way to maintenance hangars of Air India, Airworks India and even the Indian Air Force. Later, Huns Air with its fleet of three Vickers Viscounts, and Puskpaka Airlines with two ex-Indian Airlines SE.210 Caravelles also built their own hangars. The first international carrier to operate services to Bombay was Trans World Airlines, as early as January 5, 1947. A year later, on March 16, 1948, Air India's first Lockheed L-749 Constellation, VT-CQS (Mughal Princess), landed at Bombay Airport.

Despite several extensions and modifications, Santa Cruz Airport was reaching its operational capacity. To meet the constant growth in traffic and passengers, and with the future in mind, the Indian Government set up a Committee in 1967 under the chairmanship of JRD Tata to look into the issue. The Committee recommended construction of a new international terminal that would cope with additional traffic well into the 21st century. Santa Cruz would only handle domestic traffic henceforth. The new terminal later came to be known as "Sahar".

The 1970s and 80s saw a surge of airlines serving Bombay Airport. Besides the three Indian operators – Air India, Indian Airlines, and the newly-formed low-cost carrier Vayudoot – a variety of international airlines operated scheduled services to Sahar, such as Air Canada, Air France, Air Lanka, Air Mauritius, Aeroflot, Alitalia, Biman Bangladesh, British Airways, Cathay Pacific, CSA, Egyptair, Ethiopian Airlines, Gulf Air, Iran Air, Iraqi Airways, Lufthansa, Pan American, PIA, SIA, Syrian Air, Qantas and Zambia Airways to name a few. Business jets and biz-props, cargo aircraft, military operators and VIP visitors completed the busy scene. RAF transports also made Bombay a regular transit halt on their way to the Far East.

Today, Mumbai Airport handles around 44 domestic and international carriers as well as over 20 cargo operators. The new Corporate Aviation Terminal (also known as the General Aviation Terminal) opposite the domestic passenger terminal handles all executive flights. Jet Airways had its hangar and maintenance facility built close to the Air Works hangar and Indamer Co. has also built their modern facility here.

By the end of 2014, the CSIA will have undergone a sea-change, and will compare to some of the best airports in the world. But as air traffic increases the world over, even CSIA will feel a capacity crunch in the near future. A site for the construction of a new airport across the harbor is already selected. Called Navi Mumbai, or New Mumbai Airport, the construction work is yet to commence. With legal and environmental problems facing the new site, only time will tell how long one will have to wait for the new airport. Until then, enjoy the pictures of the current two airports – past and present!

HISTORIC

IN-319, L-1049C Constellation, Indian Navy
This aircraft was formerly BG582 of Indian Air Force, and VT-DGM of Air India. It was transferred to the navy on 18 November 1976, when the defence ministry decided to transfer the 'Super Connies' from the air force, for maritime duties with the Navy.

VT-CCC, Douglas C-47A, Trans Sharjah
The red and white DC-3 of Trans Sharjah noted derelict at Bombay.

VT-DIB, Douglas C-54A, Indian Airlines
Noted lying derelict outside Air Works India hangar in faded Indian Airlines colours

VT-DOE, Vickers Viscount 779D, Huns Air
Huns Air's first Viscount, purchased from Indian Airlines to carry passengers and cargo to the Gulf states.
It has a broad red cheat line with a yellow top. Named simply 'SS', and seen posing for a photo outside
the hangar.

VT-DUP, Douglas C-47B, The Hindu
Owned by The Hindu newspaper. Seen undergoing maintenance at the Air Works India hangar.

VT-CGR, Douglas C-47A, National Remote Sensing Agency
In the early days of Bombay, later Mumbai, the DC-3 and its wartime equivalent, the C-47 (seen here) were commonplace.

VT-DOH, Vickers Viscount 779D, ex-Indian Airlines
Another Huns Air Viscount hiding in the hangar

VT-DVI, SE.210 Caravelle 6N, Indian Airlines
Indian Airlines had a fleet of the classic early twinjet airliner the Sud Aviacion Caravelle. They were a regular sight at Bombay.

552, BAC One Eleven 485, Royal Oman Air Force
Receiving attention on an official visit is this One Eleven from the Royal Oman Air Force.

Boeing 707-300, Alyemda
An Alyemda 707 flanked by Indian Oil tankers noted sometime in 1980. Note the old Bombay terminal building with its control tower in the background.

VT-DFM, Douglas C-47A, Airworks India
A C-47 formerly operated by Indian Airlines, and now with Air Works India. Note the faded 'Indian Airlines' titles in hindi.

N772FT, Douglas DC-8-63F, Air India Cargo
Air India Cargo leased this DC-8 from Flying Tiger Line in 1980. It is seen in all white colours and red titles in October 1982.

VT-EHN, Airbus A300B4-203
Docked at an aerobridge, Air India has operated numerous Airbus A300 aircraft over the years.

OK-JBI, Ilyushin IL-62M, CSA
CSA's classic 'OK Jet' scheme on one of the airline's IL-62 aircraft visits Bombay in August 1982.

VT-DJK & VT-DNY, Boeing 707-437, Air India
VT-DJK, named 'Everest', and VT-DNY, named ' Dhaulagiri', face the breaker's axe, along with sistership 'DNZ outside the company's hangar in November 1983. All three were finally broken up circa 1984.

JA8542, Douglas DC-10-40, Japan Air Lines
Seen arriving with the Japanese Prime Minister. Note the flag flying from the cockpit window.

VT-CTV, Douglas C-47A, Indian Government Department Of Civil Aviation
Following a fresh coat of paint in early 1984, one of the C-47's still operating in India at the time.

VT-DXN, BAe 748-224, Indian Airlines
Although wearing Indian Airlines' livery, this aircraft is operated by regional carrier Vayudoot. It is operating a flight to Kandla.

VT-DXT, Boeing 707-337C, Air India
Seen parked on a Santa Cruz ramp at Mumbai Airport.

3B-NAF, Boeing 707-344B, Air Mauritius
Awaiting passengers for its return flight to Mauritius in the early 1980s.

G-BMEO, Short SD360-200, Thai Airways
Passing through on a delivery flight to Thai Airways and still wearing its British registration. It later took up the markings HS-TSE.

NZ7272, Boeing 727-22C, Royal New Zealand Air Force
A Boeing 727 of New Zealand's 40 Squadron on a VIP visit to Mumbai.

VT-CES, Beech 18, J K Chemicals Ltd
Spotted basking in the hot sun, the Beech 18 was commonly known as the Twin Beech.

VT-EIP, Dornier 228-201, Vayudoot
Vayudoot was set up jointly between Air India and Indian Airlines to operate regional flights.

PH-PBX, Fokker F-28-1000, Government of The Netherlands
A royal visit from The Netherlands using one of the country's indigenous aircraft, the Fokker F-28.

TC-JCS, Airbus A310-203, THY Turkish Airlines
A Turkish visitor on a VIP visit using an early Airbus A310 of the national carrier.

ZE701, BAe 146 CC2, Royal Air Force
Operated by the RAF's 32 squadron, awaiting the arrival of the Duke and Duchess of Kent for its flight back to the UK.

EI-BZU, Douglas DC-8-71, Kenya Airways
After 20 years flying for United Airlines, this DC-8 was leased by Kenya Airways. Seen arriving on runway 09 from Nairobi.

5Y-BBI, Boeing 707-351B, Kenya Airways
Kenya Airways also operated the Boeing 707 into Mumbai for a number of years.

OD-AGX, Boeing 707-327C, TMA of Lebanon
One of the classic liveries of the Middle East, TMA of Lebanon was a cargo airline which operated Boeing 707s until it ceased operations in 2004. In 2010 the airline relaunched operations with an Airbus A300.

VT-ROY, Fokker F-27-100, Goa Way/Continental
A Fokker F-27 flying for Goa Way, but operated by Continental Airlines. Jimmy was invited by the airline to fly on its inaugural flight to Goa.

CS-TEU, Boeing 737-2K9, Damania Airlines
Still wearing the registration CS-TEU of its previous operator, this Boeing 737 arrived in the last week of February 1993 and later became VT-PDB.

VH-FNF, Fokker 50, Rajair
An Australian Fokker 50 seen on arrival. It was later reregistered VT-RAB.

VT-ERX, Piper PA-31 Navajo
A Piper Navajo used for charter work by Continental Airlines.

VT-EBW, Piper PA-25-260 Pawnee C
Lying derelict outside the Air Works hangar, still faintly wearing the Airworks India titles of its former owner.

DOMESTIC

VT-EGF, Boeing 737-2A8, Alliance Air
This aircraft began operations with Indian Airlines in the early 1980s, before transferring to its subsidiary, Alliance Air, in the 1990s. It was subsequently converted into a freighter for service with Air India Cargo, ferrying freight around the country. Seen here operating for Alliance Air.

VT-EPP, Airbus A320-231, Indian Airlines
This aircraft served Indian Airlines for 22 years before being broken up at Mumbai in 2010.

VT-EPT, Airbus A320-231, Indian Airlines
A rare double-bogeyed A320 airframe, developed especially for Indian Airlines.

VT-ADZ, Airbus A320-232, Air Deccan
One among the many hybrid liveries sported by the low cost, no frills airline Air Deccan. It later merged with Kingfisher in 2008.

VT-JCJ, ATR-72 212A, Jet Airways
A Jet Airways ATR-72 making its way onto Taxiway A4 being followed closely by a much larger company Boeing 777.

VT-JGN, Boeing 737-83N, Jet Airways
One of the newer airframes flying for Jet Airways, seen here in beautiful morning light.

VT-SAY, Boeing 737-382, JetLite India
JetLite, formerly Air Sahara, was a low cost airline based at Mumbai before merging with Jet Konnect in 2012. VT-SAY parked outside the Jet Airways hangar.

VT-SPV, Boeing 737-86N, SpiceJet
On short final for runway 27, this aircraft has transferred between Transavia and SpiceJet several times.

VT-IGJ, Airbus A320-232, IndiGo
One of the newer airframes flying for IndiGo - one of India's most successful low cost carrier to date.

VT-EPK, Airbus A320-231, Air India
Painted for World AIDS Day '07, this A320 is one of the most unique and easily recognisable airframes which flew for Air India.

VT-WAB, Airbus A320-232, Go Air
Shortly before landing on runway 09, and sporting a borrowed blue engine cowling from one of its stablemates in the Go Air fleet, is A320 VT-WAB.

VT-WAG, Airbus A320-214, Go Air
Go Air's deep blue scheme on an A320 with CFM engines, seconds before departing from runway 27.

VT-WAB, Airbus A320-232, Go Air
The orange A320 - one of Go Air's most popular schemes. Stored on apron Lima due to technical reasons.

VT-WAD, Airbus A320-233, Go Air
One of the variety of colours chosen by Go Air for its A320 fleet.

VT-ESA, Airbus A320-231, Air India
An Air India A320 wearing the hybrid livery, which was not popular amongst passengers and enthusiasts.

VT-JCG, ATR-72 212A, Jet Airways
VT-JCG undergoing general maintenance outside the hangar. Notice the Konnect titles, indicating the Jet Airways subsidiary it flies for.

Airbus A319 and A320, Kingfisher Airlines
The ongoing financial difficulties at Kingfisher Airlines has meant a number of the airline's aircraft being stored on apron Lima over recent years.

VT-SAS, Canadair Regional Jet 200ER, JetLite
Air Sahara bought this aircraft from British Airline Flybe in 2003. The airline later became Jetlite India.

VT-KFN Airbus A321-232, Kingfisher Airlines
Stored at Mumbai, with a thick coat of dust on top bearing testimony to the duration of time it has remained inactive.

VT-EPP Airbus A320-231, Indian Airlines
Being broken up at Mumbai after almost 23 years of service with Indian Airlines.

MILITARY

VT-ELX, DHC-6-300 Twin Otter, Geological Survey of India
A veteran Twin Otter of the Geological Survey of India. Striking a pose on the private aviation ramp at Mumbai.

CR860, Antonov AN-32B, Sri Lankan Air Force
An extremely rare visitor to Mumbai from the Sri Lankan Air Force, seen prior to departure.

CG-773, Dornier 228-101, Indian Coast Guard
A Dornier 228 built on licence in India by HAL. On short final for runway 27.

BH1013, BAe 748-203, Indian Air Force
Hindustan Aeronautics licence-built the BAe 748 in India, with examples, such as this one, joining the Indian Air Force

BH1048, BAe 748-203, Indian Air Force
Christmas Day, another HAL-built 748 flying for the Indian Air Force.

HS-CMV, Boeing 737-4Z6, Government of Thailand
A regular visitor is this Boeing 737 of the Government of Thailand. Rumor has it that the crown prince flies it himself.

HS-CMV, Boeing 737-4Z6, Government of Thailand
The same Thai Boeing 737 seen taking off on a hot day in Mumbai.

K2413, Boeing 737-2A8, Indian Air Force
K2413 was built in 1983 for the Indian Air Force and is used as VIP transport for the Prime Minister and President.

K3013, Ilyushin IL-76MD, Indian Air Force
A noisy IL-76 heading for departure past one of the best vantage points at Mumbai Airport.

ZH103, Boeing 707 E-3D/AEW.1, Royal Air Force
Visiting India as part of Indo-UK Air Force Exercise Indradhanush, held at Air Force Station Kalaikunda, in West Medinipur district, West Bengal from October to November 2010.

04-4135, C-17 Globemaster 3A, US Air Force
Part of the large fleet of aircraft that accompanied US President Barrack Obama on his maiden trip to India. On very short final for runway 09.

K3604, Embraer 135 Legacy 600, Indian Air Force
On short finals to runway 32

KAF325, Lockheed 100 Hercules, Kuwait Air Force
Seen on what Sean describes as "The most memorable day of my life. A plethora of AN-124s, C130s, MD11s, B747Fs visited BOM!"

95-180, Lockheed C-130H Hercules, Republic of Korea Air Force
The SKAF frequents Mumbai often, mostly on fuel stops.

F-RAJA/075, Airbus A340-212, French Air Force
The French President arrived in Mumbai to pay homage to victims of the 26/11 terror attacks in 2008.

HELICOPTERS

IN 553, Westland Sea King 42A, Indian Navy
Seen in May 1986, awaiting a senior naval officer.

Z2394, Mil Mi-17, Indian Air Force
An armed Mi-17 of the IAF seen at an air show in Mumbai.

VT-ELL, Aérospatiale SA-365N Dauphin 2, Pawan Hans
Dogs, grass cutters, and a chopper! Making its way out on an active runway 08-26. It can only happen in India!

VT-JVS, Bell 206-L4, B G Shirke Construction Technology
Lifting off from Mumbai with a few domestic tails in the background.

Z2848, Aérospatiale SA 318 Alouette II, Indian Air Force
This IAF helicopter is seen on a rare visit to Mumba in March 2008.

Dogs rest on the main runway undeterred by the two noisy choppers behind - **VT-ENX** and **VT-ELI** of Pawan Hans Helicopters.

VT-AZA, Bell 412 HP, Global Vectra Helicorp
Lifting off on a hot day.

VT-ASM, Mil Mi-172, Pawan Hans Helicopters
Coming in to land from a sortie in October 2002.

CARGO

Antonov AN-12B, Meridian
A stunning cargo surprise at Mumbai, Sean comments "I held vigil for four hours to photograph this aircraft departing."

N526UP, Boeing 747-212B(F), Tradewinds Airlines
Wearing a hybrid livery, this Tradewinds Airlines Boeing 747 arrives at Mumbai.

VT-EJH, Airbus A310-304(F), Air India Cargo
Various aircraft, including this A310, receive attention outside an Air India hangar.

ET-AJX, Boeing 757-260(PCF), Ethiopian Airlines Cargo
Wearing '60 years' titles to celebrate the Diamond Anniversary of Ethiopian Airlines.

B-2178, McDonnell Douglas MD-11(F), Shanghai Airlines Cargo
Holding short of runway 27, one of the regular cargo operators to Mumbai.

RA-76950, Ilyushin IL-76TD-90, Volga-Dnepr Airlines
'IL-76 'Vladimir Kokkinaki' climbing out of runway 27 with upgraded, quieter, turbofans - a huge difference from the usual sound of an IL-76 on departure.

RA-76951, Ilyushin IL-76TD-90, Volga-Dnepr Airlines
A stunning Ilyushin IL-76 of Volga-Dnepr Airlines poses head-on for the camera.

B-HUP, Boeing 747-467F, Cathay Pacific Cargo
A hive of activity surrounds this Boeing 747 freighter of Cathay Pacific Cargo on turnaround.

D-ACGB, Boeing 747-409BDSF, Air Cargo Germany
Pictured on a night halt ready to be pushed back, Air Cargo Germany operates large Boeing 747-400 freighters on flights around the world, including Mumbai.

N760SA, Boeing 747-230B(F), Southern Air
Throwing up masses of spray as its engines spool up for departure, and wearing the latest Southern Air livery.

N705GC, McDonnell Douglas MD-11F, Gemini Air Cargo
A Gemini Air Cargo pilot takes a photograph in return prior to departure.

VT-FFA, BAe ATP, First Flight Couriers
First Flight Couriers was a short-lived domestic cargo carrier, utilising BAe ATP freighters.

UP-AN212, Antonov AN-12B, ATMA
Four beautiful blue buzzing props on very short final for runway 14.

UP-AN213, Antonov AN-12BP, ATMA
Pictured moments from touchdown on runway 27. ATMA always sports blue propellers.

N601FE, McDonnell Douglas MD-11F, FedEx Express
One of the older aircraft now flying across the Atlantic, this MD-11 freighter is seen on very short finals for runway 09 with the famous Western Express Highway below.

N278UP, McDonnell Douglas MD-11(F), UPS
The monsoon is in full swing as this UPS trijet glides in. Notice the vapour trails due to the humidity. In the background is another workhorse of yesteryear - the A300 of Indian Airlines awaiting its fate.

RA-76783, Ilyushin IL-76TD, Atlant-Soyuz Airlines
Screaming overhead on approach to runway 27. The Ilyushin IL-76 is one of the noisier aircraft to use Mumbai Airport.

UR-ZYD, Antonov AN-124, Maximus Air
The massive AN-124 awaiting departure clearance on taxiway A4. Maximus usually sends the A300F to Mumbai, but this day saw a welcome change.

VT-BDH, Boeing 737-25C(F), Blue Dart Aviation
India's largest cargo and logistics company operates a mix of Boeing 737 and 757 freighters.

VT-BDK, Boeing 757-236(SF), Blue Dart Aviation
Dubbed the 'Pencil' freighter, a Blue Dart Boeing 757 heads for departure.

A7-AFB, Airbus A300B4-622R(F), Qatar Airways Cargo
Qatar Airways Cargo A300 powering down after having just arrived on stand, loaded with cargo.

VT-EGF, Boeing 737-2A8(F), Air India Cargo
This aircraft began operations with Indian Airlines back in the early 1980s. It then went to subsidiary Alliance Air in the 1990s, and subsequently was converted to a freighter for service with Air India Cargo, ferrying freight around the country.

VT-EQS, Airbus A310-304(F), Air India Cargo
'Air India A310 'Krishna' waits for her turn on to the active runway as a Global Supply Systems Boeing 747 roars down runway 27.

RA-82074, Antonov AN-124-100, Volga-Dnepr Airlines
Pushed back, the crew are about to close the rear ramp door of this mammoth AN-124 of Volga-Dnepr Airlines.

CHARTER/VIP

RA-96019, Ilyushin IL-96-300, Russian Government
Part of the aircraft fleet that brought Russian President Dmitry Medvedev to India on his visit in December 2010.

RA-96019, Ilyushin IL-96-300, Russian Government
A Russian Government IL-96 parked at the International Terminal during a visit of the Russian President.

G-OJIB, Boeing 757-28A, Astraeus Airlines/Iron Maiden
The stunning 'ED FORCE ONE' - IRON MAIDEN'S private Boeing 757 on her way out of Mumbai bound for Perth - the next destination on the 'Somewhere Back in Time World Tour' during 2008. The group kickstarted this tour with the first show in Mumbai, and the aircraft is flown by the group's lead singer Bruce Dickinson.

RA-86570, Ilyushin IL-62M, Russia – Ministry for Emergency Situations (MChS)
An ultra-rare visitor to Mumbai. Sean says "I was lucky to have seen the 'Follow Me' jeep escort this vintage beauty onto the runway."

JY-JAV, Airbus A310-222, Jordan Aviation/United Nations
The United Nations sub-leased this Jordanian Aviation A310 in 2008. Seen vacating runway 09 three days after the deadly Mumbai terror attacks.

G-BZAV, Avro RJ100
RJ100 wearing its former British registration, on a fuel stop in Mumbai heading for a new life in Australia.

Challenger 604, DB Group
The stunning lines of a Challenger, striking a pose on the General Aviation ramp.

VT-KBN, Raytheon 390 Premier 1, Span Air
Span Air is a private air charter operator that provides helicopters and business jets on hire and lease. Seen seconds from touchdown against the hectic construction cranes at the new International Integrated Terminal.

VT-RSB, Beech King Air B200, Greaves Travel
Belonging to luxury travel and tour company Greaves Travel on the General Aviation ramp. Sean: "I had the pleasure of flying onboard this little beauty from Mumbai all the way to Delhi."

JA13AN, Boeing 737-781ER, ANA BusinessJet
The regular All Nippon Airways business jet that flies from Tokyo-Mumbai, with a technical stop in Fukuoka.

TC-MEN, Learjet 60
Being escorted by the 'Follow Me' jeep to runway 27 for departure.

VT-JSE, Challenger 300, JSW Steel Ltd
Belonging to one of India's industrial powerhouses - JSW Steel.

VT-JVL, Beech King Air B200, Jaypee Ventures
A panning shot of this Beech King Air. "Bizprops and Bizjets are the most challenging aircraft to shoot while in motion!"

VT-TET, Rinaldo-Piaggio Avanti RP-180 II, Taj Air
The unusual shape of the Avanti, operated by Taj Air, a charter operator from Delhi.

VT-LJS, Beech King Air 350B, Bharat Hotels Ltd
A Beech King Air operated by the Bharat Hotels Group.

N707JT, Boeing 707-138B, John Travolta/QANTAS
This page and next. Sean comments "I couldn't have dreamed of a better birthday present than John Travolta visiting Mumbai to launch a range of Breitling watches, and flying in none other than his own immaculate Boeing 707!" He adds "It was expected to arrive two days earlier, but our intrepid vigil for three long days to spot this stunner arrive and depart was well worth the effort! The closeup of the nose shows titles 'Jett Clipper Ella' - named after his children Jett and Ella Bleu Travolta."

N707JT, Boeing 707-138B, John Travolta/QANTAS
Glistening in the September sun with a Kingfisher aircraft departing behind

N727VJ, Boeing 727-44(QWS), Kingfisher Airlines
The 1966 classic Boeing 727 is owned by United Breweries and appears in full Kingfisher colours.

AIRPORT

Mumbai Airport Tower
Mumbai Airport Air Traffic Control (ATC) Tower

Runway 27 Approach Lights

Spotting at Mumbai
Jimmy caught in action composing a picture of an incoming Saudi Air Cargo Boeing 747 freighter.

Indian Airliners
The remote parking bay showcasing an array of tails while routine maintenance is carried out on taxiway A4.

Terminal 1A
The domestic terminal 1A with the rapid exit taxiways N9 and N10 under construction in the foreground.

Terminal 2
International Terminal 2 undergoing redevelopment to create a new ultra-modern facility. Note the signature Mumbai taxis parked below.

Mumbai Terminal 1C

Terminal 1C Interior

Jet Airways Stands
The entire range of Jet Airways' fleet types on the remote apron - from the mighty Boeing 777-300ER to the Airbus A330-200 and baby Boeing 737.

Waiting For Departure
The morning departure rush hour.

Sunrise at Mumbai Airport

Terminal 1C

JUHU AERODROME

VT-CUH, Beech D-18S, Tata Services
Outside the hangar at Juhu in 1986.

VT-EFA, Beech 58P Baron, Government of Rajasthan
Parked outside the hangar.

VT-CGA, Douglas C-47A, Airworks India
Air Works India ferried their DC3 from Santacruz to Juhu for the air show with additional "50 Years in World Aviation" titles.

VT-EBW, Piper PA-25-260 Pawnee C
Another beauty from the Air Works stable gives some shade to the two policemen guarding it at the air show.

Juhu Aerodrome Helicopters
A few helicopters belonging to Global Vectra Helicorp parked outside the ONGC hangar.

VT-NWG, Cessna 152
This aircraft belongs to the Nagpur Flying Club, but has been leased by Bombay Flying Club to cover a shortage of training aircraft.

Juhu Runway 26
The main runway 08-26 leading to the famous Juhu beach with the Arabian Sea in the distance.

Juhu Tower
Juhu's iconic vanilla ice cream cone ATC tower.

Airline offices and hangars inside the aerodrome seen after a heavy monsoon shower

INTERNATIONAL

VT-AXZ, Boeing 737-8HG, Air India Express
Featuring a traditional scene on the well-known Dal Lake in Kashmir.

VT-AXP, Boeing 737-8HG, Air India Express
One of the many unique schemes worn by Air India Express aircraft, this time showing a lady playing the traditional Swarbat musical instrument.

VT-AXT, Boeing 737-8HG, Air India Express
Featuring the Painted Stork tail livery.

VT-AYC, Boeing 737-8HG, Air India Express
Featuring the famous handmade Pataola Saree which originates from Gujarat.

VT-AXR, Boeing 737-8HG, Air India Express
Featuring the Vallam Kali – the traditional paddled war canoe race in Kerala.

VT-AXJ, Boeing 737-8HG, Air India Express
Busy technicians working on the cockpit glass of this baby Boeing.

VT-EPX, Boeing 747-337, Air India
After serving the national carrier for around 20 years, this beauty was broken up in 2009 at Kemble in the UK. Seen here in 2008 ready for departure.

VT-EPW, Boeing 747-337, Air India
Another 23 year old workhorse seen undergoing maintenace checks at Mumbai in 2008. It was later broken up at the airport.

VT-EPW, Boeing 747-337, Air India
Air India engineers peering into the GE fan blades during maintenance checks of this classic Boeing 747.

RA-96010, Ilyushin IL-96-300, Aeroflot
Due to extreme fog at Delhi, this Russian IL-96 diverted in to Mumbai where the weather was much brighter.

JY-AYF, Airbus A320-232, Royal Jordanian Airlines
The evening light enhances the classic colour scheme of Royal Jordanian's Airbus A320.

A4O-GJ, Boeing 767-3P6ER, Gulf Air
Seen on very short finals for runway 27, this Boeing 767 is painted in special colours marking the 50th anniversary of Gulf Air.

A40-BU, Boeing 737-81M, Oman Air
Awaiting its turn while neighbouring Yemenia rolls down runway 27.

VT-ESP, Boeing 747-437, Air India
Air India has operated the Boeing 747-400 since 1993, using the type to launch service to New York.

N702DN, Boeing 777-232LR, Delta
Usually operating during the hours of darkness at Mumbai, Delta's Boeing 777-200LR is seen in daylight following a delay.

SU-GDB, Boeing 737-866, Egypt Air
Sporting the attractive new livery of Egypt Air and waiting for departure clearance.

VH-EBI, Airbus A330-203, QANTAS
How many A330s can you count? A different scene from the usual Boeing dominance at Mumbai.

4R-ABJ, Airbus A320-232, SriLankan Airlines
An A320 wearing the 'Visit Sri lanka 2011' titles, on short finals for runway 27.

Airbus A340-313X, Turkish Airlines
The runway direction changes, with the first departure being a stunning Turkish Airbus A340.

TC-JDA, Airbus A310-304, Turkish Airlines
A dawn shot of Turkish Airbus A310 'Erzurum' on its way to departure.

G-VGAL, Boeing 747-443, Virgin Atlantic Airways
Virgin replaced the usual Airbus A340 on their London route with the Boeing 747-400, giving opportunity for this arrival shot.

D-AIHQ, Airbus A340-642X, Lufthansa
Another substitute, with Lufthansa sending the longer Airbus A340-600 over their usual -300.

ZS-JAV, Fokker F-28-4000, Myanma Airways
Seen on a fuel stop heading for a new life with Myanma Airways, this rare Fokker F-28 transits Mumbai from its previous life in South Africa.

A9C-KE, Airbus A330-243, Gulf Air
Waiting for departure clearance. Notice the unusual Sri Lankan Airlines decals on the RR Trent engine cowling.

VT-AIS, Boeing 747-4H6, Air India
This Air India Boeing 747-4H6 formerly flew with Malaysia Airlines before joining Air India. It is seen holding on Alpha 4 for departure clearance.

ET-AKC, Boeing 757-260, Ethiopian Airlines
A detail shot of an Ethiopian Airlines Boeing 757 wearing very colorful 'Celebrating Ethiopia's Millenium' stickers.

EP-IAG, Boeing 747-286B, Iran Air
A 1976 classic, Iran Air is one of the few airlines still flying the Boeing 747-200 model today.

VT-EVB, Boeing 747-437, Air India
The Maharajah standing proud in the hot mumbai winter sun, with its doors open to keep the cabin temperature down.

4X-EAC, Boeing 767-258ER, El Al
The recognisable livery of El Al is seen on this Boeing 767-200 model, arriving from Tel Aviv.

VT-EPW, Boeing 747-337, Air India
The four GE engines of this Boeing 747-337 demonstrate their impressive thrust on a rainy day.

9M-XAA, Airbus A330-301, Air Asia X
Caught roaring off runway 14 on a clear day and wearing a fantastic livery showcasing the wonders of the modern world. An Air Asia X Airbus A330 heading for Kuala Lumpur.

VT-AXT, Boeing 737-8HG, Air India Express
6.47pm. Air India Express Boeing 737 being pushed back for a departure in warm evening light.

VT-JWP, Airbus A330-202, Jet Airways
In the hours of darkness, Mumbai is still a hive of activity. A Jet Airways A330 is caught on the ramp.

VT-JEG, Boeing 777-35RER, Jet Airways
Jet Airways' Boeing 777 Echo Golf 's rudder is given some serious attention by the airline's technical team.

A6-EIA, Airbus A320-232, Etihad Airways
A late night departure to Abu Dhabi - Etihad Airways is one of the Middle East's airline success stories.

VT-ANH, Boeing 787-8 Dreamliner, Air India
The very first Dreamliner flies in to Mumbai with spirit and bonhomie, beckoning with its large raked wingtips outstretched.

VT-ANH, Boeing 787-8 Dreamliner, Air India
The traditional water canon salute welcoming Air India's first Boeing 787 on her maiden visit to Mumbai, in 2012.

Mumbai Airports through time